CREATE THE CODE

COMPUTER GRAPHICS

Max Wainewright

WAYLAND
www.waylandbooks.co.uk

First published in Great Britain in 2020
by Wayland

Credits:
Editor: Elise Short
Designer: Matt Lilly
Cover Design: Peter Scoulding
Illustrations: John Haslam

HB ISBN: 978 1 5263 1360 7
PB ISBN: 978 1 5263 1361 4

Printed and bound in Dubai

Picture credits:

Devrimb/iStock:5c; Christos Georghiou/
Shutterstock: 1tl, 4br; Gorodenkoff/
Shutterstock: 21cr; Maxiphoto/iStock: 4tl;
Finlay McWalter/PD/Wikimedia Commons:
5t; OktalStudio/iStock: 21cl; Angy Vaks/
Shutterstock: 21t.

Every attempt has been made
to clear copyright. Should there be any
inadvertent omission please apply to
the publisher for rectification.

Wayland
An imprint of
Hachette Children's Group
Part of Hodder and Stoughton
Carmelite House
50 Victoria Embankment
London EC4Y 0DZ

An Hachette UK Company
www.hachette.co.uk
www.hachettechildrens.co.uk

Contents

Computer Graphics 4

Drawing with Code 6

3D Name 8

Painting 10

Special FX 12

Text-based Coding 14

HTML Stripes 16

Shape Art 18

How do Screens
    Display Graphics? 20

Coding 3D Graphics 21

Introducing X3D 22

X3D Tree 24

X3D Forest 26

X3D Solar System 27

The Scratch Screen/
Glossary 30

Bugs & Debugging 31

Index 32

For help with any of the projects go to: www.maxw.com

Computer Graphics

Computer graphics are images or designs that are created using a computer. They can be found everywhere: on your phone, your computer, in films and video games.

The first computers couldn't actually display any pictures – only numbers. As technology developed, programmers used squares and lines to create simple images. They had very few colours to choose from as computer screens could only display black and white or black and green. As computers got faster and more powerful the quality of their graphics improved.

One of the first computer games was Pong, created in 1972. Players used controls to bounce a ball across the screen in this tennis-like game.

▮ Colour

As computer technology evolved, so did the number of colours computer screens could display: in the 1970s they went from 16 to 32 different colours. Today's computer screens can display over 16 million colours. Find out how to use code to set colours on page 20.

▮ Pixel size

Early computer graphics were very 'chunky' because they were made out of large squares called pixels (short for picture element). In the early 1980s, some computers could display 3,000 pixels - now even mobile phones have over 1,000,000 pixels.

Help! I'm becoming pixelated!

Speed

By 1974, computer graphics had developed enough to draw realistic objects like *The Utah Teapot* (see right). But it took a computer several hours to render (draw) a fully detailed teapot. Rendering the teapot today would take milliseconds. More sophisticated images, such as the ones created for animated films, can take almost a day to render a single frame. Each second of a film contains 24 frames: that's a lot of time spent rendering images! Start coding your own 3D graphics on page 21.

Special effects

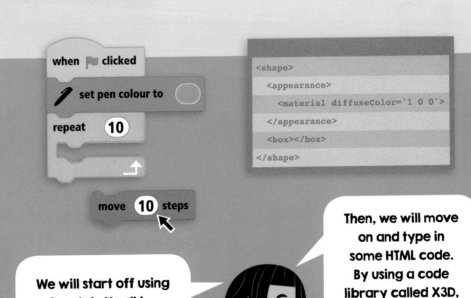

As computer graphics become more and more sophisticated, it's hard to tell what is real and what has been created by a computer. Real-world images can now be combined with computer graphics to create new experiences called augmented reality (AR) and virtual reality (VR). We'll be learning how explosions are created using CGI (computer generated images) on pages 12-13.

Coding

There are lots of programs and apps available to help you create your own graphics. You can use a mouse to draw shapes or even design 3D houses. But in this book, we will be using code to create graphics. You'll learn how to create shapes, set colours, make a simple drawing program and work with 3D objects. As well as learning the code you'll discover how some of the technologies involved actually work.

```
when ⚑ clicked
✏ set pen colour to ◯
repeat 10

        ↑
```

```
move 10 steps
```

```
<shape>
  <appearance>
    <material diffuseColor='1 0 0'>
  </appearance>
  <box></box>
</shape>
```

We will start off using Scratch. You'll be dragging blocks of code around to create your own graphics programs.

Then, we will move on and type in some HTML code. By using a code library called X3D, we'll explore 3D coding.

Drawing with Code

All coding languages use commands to create graphics. Let's get started with Scratch.

STEP 1: Start Scratch

Open your browser and type in **scratch.mit.edu**

Press the **enter** key.

Click **Create** to get started.

STEP 2: The pen

We need to add extra code blocks that let us draw while the code is running. This group of code blocks is called an extension.

Click the **Add Extension** icon.

Click on **Pen**.

STEP 3: Get coding

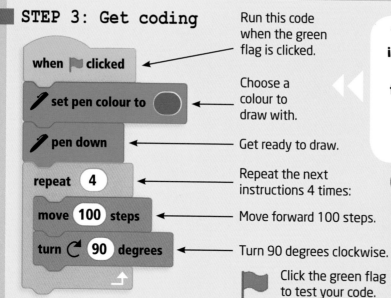

Run this code when the green flag is clicked.

Choose a colour to draw with.

Get ready to draw.

Repeat the next instructions 4 times:

Move forward 100 steps.

Turn 90 degrees clockwise.

Click the green flag to test your code.

To choose a colour in Scratch, click the rounded square, then use the sliders to choose the shade you want.

We'll learn more advanced ways to set colours later in the book.

How big is a step in Scratch?

All coding languages handle graphics by using a grid of pixels.

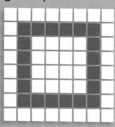

Shapes are drawn on the stage by changing the colour of specific pixels. The stage is the white area in the top right of the Scratch screen.

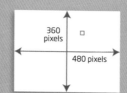

360 pixels

480 pixels

In Scratch, the stage is normally 480 pixels wide and 360 pixels high. Scratch calls each pixel a step.

If you click the **Full screen** button, everything gets much bigger. But the stage is still treated as being 480 x 360 steps.

STEP 4: Experiment

Drag the cat sprite around the screen. Click the green flag to run your code again. Try changing the colour of the square and running the code.

STEP 5: Lots of squares

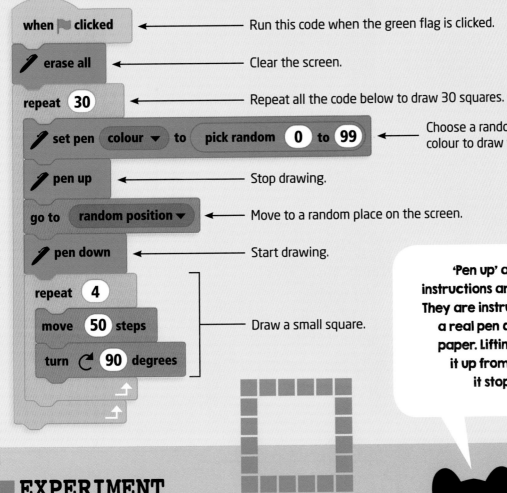

when ⚑ clicked ← Run this code when the green flag is clicked.

⬗ erase all ← Clear the screen.

repeat 30 ← Repeat all the code below to draw 30 squares.

⬗ set pen colour ▼ to (pick random 0 to 99) ← Choose a random colour to draw with.

⬗ pen up ← Stop drawing.

go to random position ▼ ← Move to a random place on the screen.

⬗ pen down ← Start drawing.

repeat 4
move 50 steps ⎤ Draw a small square.
turn ↻ 90 degrees ⎦

'Pen up' and 'pen down' instructions aren't motion blocks. They are instructions that imitate a real pen drawing on some paper. Lifting the pen up lifts it up from the paper - so it stops drawing.

EXPERIMENT

Try changing the number of steps in the move command block. What happens?

Can you find a way to draw more than 30 squares?

Drag the **set pen size** block into your code, and set the size to 5. What happens? Try other numbers.

Try changing the angle turned to 120 degrees. What shapes are drawn? Can you draw other shapes?

3D Name

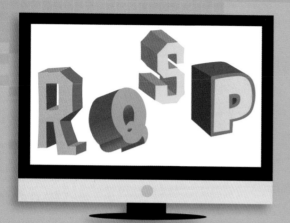

Discover how to create some impressive graphic effects. First let's draw some text on the screen in a random position. Then we'll change the colour slightly and move the text down, and to the left. This will give it a simple '3D shadow' effect.

STEP 1: Start Scratch

`scratch.mit.edu`

Start Scratch and click **Create**.

STEP 2: Add the pen extension

Click **Add Extension**.

Click **Pen**.

Pen

STEP 3: No cats

Click the blue x to delete the cat sprite.

Sprite1

STEP 4: New sprite

Hover your mouse over the **Choose sprite** button.

Paint

Move up to the **brush** icon.

Paint

Click on it.

STEP 5: Add text

Select the **Text** tool.

Click into the drawing area.

Type in your name.

Curly
Sans serif
Serif
Handwriting
Marker
Curly

Choose a font.

Click the **Select** tool.

Max

Stretch the text box to make it about half the width of the drawing area.

STEP 6: Start coding

📃 **Code**　　Click the **Code** tab then drag this code into the **Scripts** area:

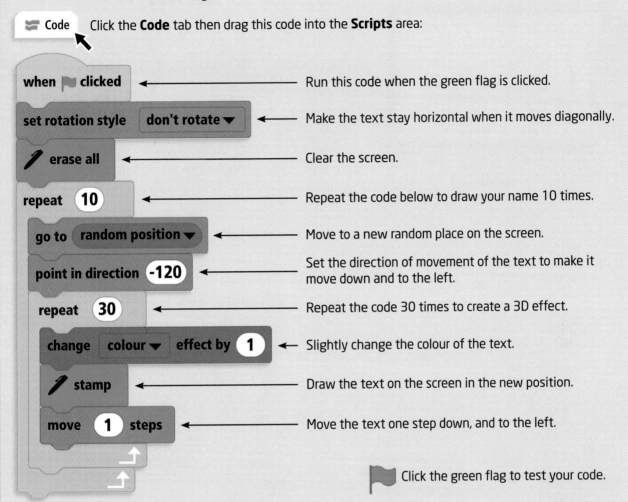

when 🚩 clicked ← Run this code when the green flag is clicked.

set rotation style **don't rotate ▼** ← Make the text stay horizontal when it moves diagonally.

✏ erase all ← Clear the screen.

repeat (10) ← Repeat the code below to draw your name 10 times.

go to (random position ▼) ← Move to a new random place on the screen.

point in direction (-120) ← Set the direction of movement of the text to make it move down and to the left.

repeat (30) ← Repeat the code 30 times to create a 3D effect.

change (colour ▼) effect by (1) ← Slightly change the colour of the text.

✏ stamp ← Draw the text on the screen in the new position.

move (1) steps ← Move the text one step down, and to the left.

🚩 Click the green flag to test your code.

◼ EXPERIMENT

Experiment with the values in the repeat loops. Try changing 10 and 30 to bigger numbers and see what happens.

Use a different value in the **change colour effect by** code block. What changes?

Instead of -120 degrees, use a different angle and see how it changes the effect.

Try using different fonts. Click on the **Costumes** tab, then choose the 'T' (text tool). Change the font and run the code again.

> Later on in the book we will learn how to create a true 3D effect.

Painting

There are lots of programs and apps that allow you to draw pictures and colour them. But how do they work?

This project will teach you how to code a simple drawing program. As the mouse is moved around, the pen block will draw a circle in your mouse's location. Extra code changes the colour of your pen, and adds symmetry to the picture.

STEP 1: Start Scratch

scratch.mit.edu

Start Scratch and click **Create**.

STEP 2: Add the pen extension

Click **Add Extension**.

Pen

Click **Pen**.

STEP 3: Start coding

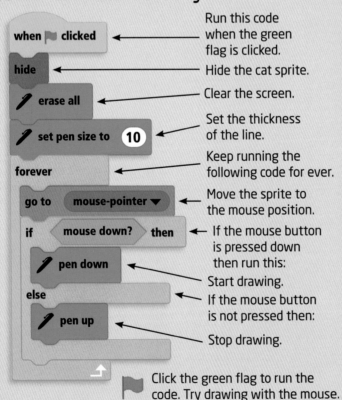

when 🏳 clicked — Run this code when the green flag is clicked.

hide — Hide the cat sprite.

🖋 erase all — Clear the screen.

🖋 set pen size to 10 — Set the thickness of the line.

forever — Keep running the following code for ever.

go to mouse-pointer ▼ — Move the sprite to the mouse position.

if mouse down? then — If the mouse button is pressed down then run this:

🖋 pen down — Start drawing.

else — If the mouse button is not pressed then:

🖋 pen up — Stop drawing.

🏳 Click the green flag to run the code. Try drawing with the mouse.

The first mouse

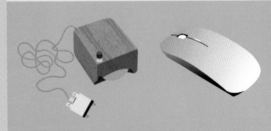

The computer mouse was invented in the 1960s by Douglas Engelbart.

The first mouse used a ball that rotated when it was moved across a desk. The ball turned tiny wheels that could detect when the mouse was being moved.

Now computer mice use optical technology: an LED shines light under the mouse onto the desk. A special sensor measures how much light is reflected back and works out how the mouse has been moved.

STEP 4: Changing colour

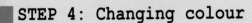

When the '**R**' key is pressed run this code:

Set the drawing colour to red.

When '**Y**' key is pressed:

Set the colour to yellow.

🚩 Click the green flag again. Try pressing the 'R' key, then drawing with the mouse. Now try the 'Y' key.

STEP 5: Experiment!

P B G O

How many different colours can you add to your program?

Repeat step 4 using different key instructions and different colours, such as pressing 'B' to start drawing with blue and so on.

STEP 6: Changing size

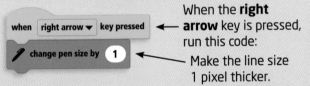

When the **right arrow** key is pressed, run this code:

Make the line size 1 pixel thicker.

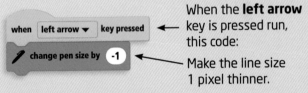

When the **left arrow** key is pressed run, this code:

Make the line size 1 pixel thinner.

🚩 Click the green flag again. Use the right and left arrow keys to make the line thicker and thinner as you draw.

STEP 7: Another brush

Right-click on the cat sprite in the **Sprites** pane.

Click **duplicate**. When you duplicate the sprite, the code gets duplicated too.

STEP 8: Edit the code

Find the **go to mouse pointer** commands and drag it out of the code.

Replace it with the **go to x y** code block. Drag in a **minus** block, a **mouse x** and **mouse y** block. This will draw another circle on the opposite side of the screen.

EXPERIMENT

What happens if you change the code in the new sprite to this:

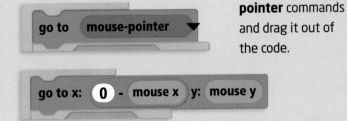

Special FX

Many films use CGI to add special effects.

When you see an explosion in a film, or a fire breathing dragon walking down a real street next to real actors, then coding has probably been involved. In this project we will make a simple explosion effect to see how this kind of code works.

STEP 1: Start Scratch

scratch.mit.edu

Start Scratch and click **Create**.

STEP 2: No cats

This is not a safe place for cats. Click the blue cross to delete the sprite.

Sprite1

STEP 3: The background

Code   **Backdrops**

Click the **Backdrops** tab.

Convert to Bitmap

Click the **Convert to Bitmap** button.

Click the **Fill** button.

Choose black.

Fill the backdrop with black.

STEP 4: Start coding

Code

Click the **Code** tab then drag in this code.

```
when stage clicked
broadcast  message1 ▼  and wait
```

> This will send a message to any sprites every time the background is clicked.

STEP 5: Set message

```
New message
message1
```

Click **message1** then select **New message**.

New message ⊗

New message name:

explode

Cancel   OK

Type **explode** then click **OK**.

> To simulate the explosion we will make lots of tiny particles. The particles will all fly apart in random directions. They will fall to the ground increasingly quickly.

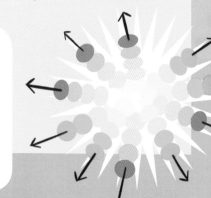

STEP 6: Add a sprite

Click the choose **new sprite** button.

Ball

Scroll through and click on **Ball**. It will be one of the particles.

STEP 7: Add a variable

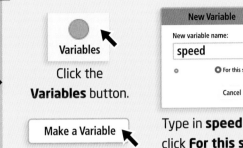

Variables

Click the **Variables** button.

Make a Variable

Click **Make a Variable**.

New Variable

New variable name:

speed

For this sprite only

Cancel OK

Type in **speed** then click **For this sprite only** then click **OK**.

STEP 8: Code the explosion

Drag in this code to create the particles, then make them explode:

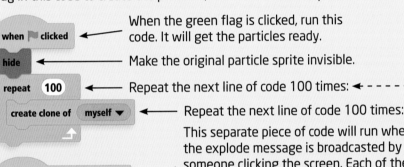

when ⚑ clicked — When the green flag is clicked, run this code. It will get the particles ready.

hide — Make the original particle sprite invisible.

repeat 100 — Repeat the next line of code 100 times: ◀------- **EXPERIMENT** with this value.

create clone of myself ▼ — Repeat the next line of code 100 times:

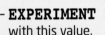

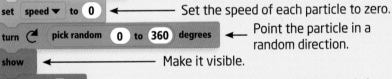

when I receive explode ▼ — This separate piece of code will run when the explode message is broadcasted by someone clicking the screen. Each of the cloned particles will run the code.

set speed ▼ to 0 — Set the speed of each particle to zero.

turn ↻ pick random 0 to 360 degrees — Point the particle in a random direction.

show — Make it visible.

set size to 30 % — Shrink it down to 30% of its normal size.

clear graphic effects — Remove any colour changes made in the repeat loop below.

go to mouse-pointer ▼ — Move it to where the screen was clicked.

repeat 30 — Repeat the following lines of code 30 times: ◀---- **EXPERIMENT** with this value.

move pick random 0 to 20 steps — Move the particle forward a random amount. ◀--- **EXPERIMENT** with these numbers.

change speed ▼ by -1 — Make the particle fall quicker.

change y by speed — Move it down to the ground quicker to simulate gravity.

change size by -1 — Make it slightly smaller.

change colour ▼ effect by pick random -5 to 2 — Change the colour a random amount. ◀----- **EXPERIMENT** with these numbers.

hide — Hide the particle when it has finished moving.

 Click the green flag to run the code. Click the screen to test the explosion.

Text-based Coding

In the next few projects we will be using more advanced coding techniques. You will need to download a program called a text editor to create the code for these projects. Always ask an adult before downloading anything.

Visit www.maxw.com for more info on downloading text editors.

STEP 1: Find the Sublime Text website

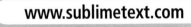

www.sublimetext.com

Sublime Text

Open your web browser and visit **www.sublimetext.com**.

STEP 2: Download

Download

Click the **Download** button near the top of the web page.

Choose the version you need.

OSX (10.7 or later)
Windows - also
Windows 64 bit

Wait for the download to be complete.

STEP 3: Install the software

Some web browsers will then ask you to run the installation program. Choose 'Run'.

Installing ...

If this does not happen, don't panic. The installer file should have been downloaded to your computer. Look in your **downloads** folder for it. Double-click on it to start installing your new text editor. You should get a grey box giving you instructions on what to do next. Follow these instructions to complete the installation.

For help go to:
www.maxw.com

STEP 4: Running Sublime Text

Open **Sublime Text** from your app list.

\<HTML>

There are over one and a half billion websites in the world. New sites are added every day, and new phones, tablets and computers are produced to view them on. For all the different web pages to be read anywhere on any device, there needs to be clearly agreed standards and codes for how to display them. HTML is the universal language that is used to create all of these web pages.

A special program called a web browser is used to view a web page. Commonly used web browsers include Google Chrome, Internet Explorer, Safari and Firefox.

HTML pages can contain different components, including images, text, tables, headings, buttons, links and videos. Each of these separate components on a page are called an element. Each element has tags and content. The tag explains what type of element to display, and the content tells the browser what to display in that element.

We will be looking at how we can make simple 2D and 3D graphics using HTML.

\<TAGS>

Tags always start with < and end with > (known as angle brackets).

All elements have an opening tag and most have a closing tag.

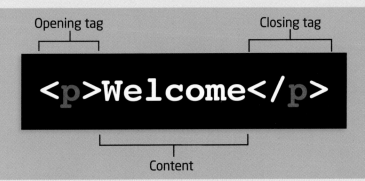

Opening tag   Closing tag

\<p>Welcome\</p>

Content

STEP 5: A simple web page

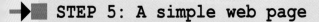

```
Sublime Text
1  <html>
2     <p>Welcome</p>
3  </html>
```

All HTML files start with \<html>.

Show a paragraph saying 'Welcome'.

All HTML files end with \</html>.

STEP 6: Save your page

■ Click **File > Save**.

■ Browse to your documents folder.

■ Type **welcome.html** as the file name.

STEP 7: View your page

■ Open your documents folder.

■ Find the **welcome.html** file and double-click on it.

■ Your web page should now load in your normal web browser.

documents/welcome.html

Welcome

You have built a simple web page. Let's learn how to add some graphics to the page.

HTML Stripes

Let's learn more about HTML.

Create some simple coloured rectangles.

Instead of using paragraphs we use an HTML element called a div - short for division.

 documents/stripes.html

A style section sets the divs' properties, such as the size of the divs.

 **<div>**

```
div{width:500px; height:50px;}
```

'Width' is a property.

The colon indicates that what comes next is the setting of the property.

Semicolons are used to separate each property.

<div>
↑
An opening div tag looks like this.

<div/>
↑
The **forward slash /** indicates the closing of the tag.

We use this code to set the colour of each individual div.

```
<div style="background-colour:blue">
```

Use an equals sign here.

Use double quotes when setting a property inside a div.

STEP 1: Start a new HTML file
Start your text editor, or click **File > New**.

Type symbols like these ">/; really carefully.

STEP 2: Type in the code

Carefully type this into your text editor.

```
1  <!DOCTYPE html>
2  <html>
3  <style>
4      div{width:500px; height:50px;}
5  </style>
6  <div style="background-colour:blue"></div>
7  <div style="background-colour:red"></div>
8  <div style="background-colour:orange"></div>
9  </html>
```

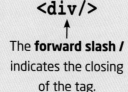

← This tells the browser that the code used is the latest version of HTML and makes sure that the web browser will understand our code.

← All HTML files start with the <html> tag.

← Start the style section.

← Set the size of each div to be 500 pixels wide and 50 pixels high.

← End the style section.

← Show a blue div.

← Show a red div.

← Show an orange div.

← This ends the HTML file.

STEP 2: Save your page

- Click **File > Save**.
- Go to your documents folder.
- Type **stripes.html** as the file name.

STEP 3: View your page

Open your documents folder and double-click on the **stripes.html** file.

documents/stripes.html

STEP 4: Arrange your screen

As you start to develop more complex HTML pages you need to be able to see your code and the HTML page at the same time. Many web developers set up their screen so the HTML is on the left-hand side and their web page is shown on the right-hand side of their screen.

Resize your text editor and browser windows so your screen looks like this:

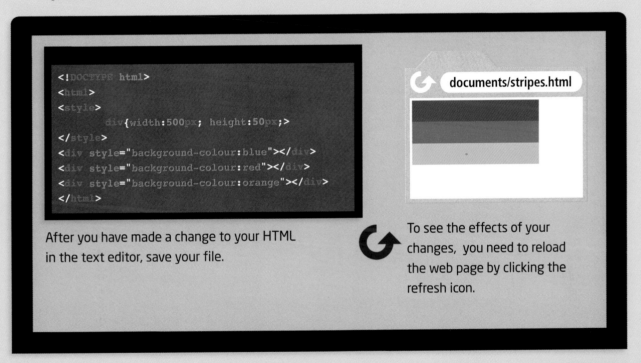

```
<!DOCTYPE html>
<html>
<style>
        div{width:500px; height:50px;>
</style>
<div style="background-colour:blue"></div>
<div style="background-colour:red"></div>
<div style="background-colour:orange"></div>
</html>
```

documents/stripes.html

After you have made a change to your HTML in the text editor, save your file.

To see the effects of your changes, you need to reload the web page by clicking the refresh icon.

EXPERIMENT

Try changing the colour of each of the divs. Remember to save and refresh your page to see the changes.

Change **height:50px** to **height:200px**. Save and refresh the page. What happens? Experiment with different values.

Try adding some more div elements to the page. Can you make a page with eight stripes? Which colours will you use?

Many flags use horizontal stripes. Find some pictures on the Internet. Can you recreate the German flag or maybe design your own.

Shape Art

Now let's make a more complex HTML page. Instead of the div elements appearing as stripes, let's position them using co-ordinates.

We need to include the 'position:absolute' command in the style section of the page, in order to use position co-ordinates to set where things go.

We also need to determine the size for each individual div by adding width and height properties to the style attribute of each div 'tag' in our code.

documents/art.html

Set the top property to specify how far down the screen each div is.

Set how far across the screen each div is by setting its left property.

■ **STEP 1: Start a new HTML file**

Start your text editor, or click **File > New**.

■ **STEP 2: Type in the HTML code**

Type this code into your text editor.

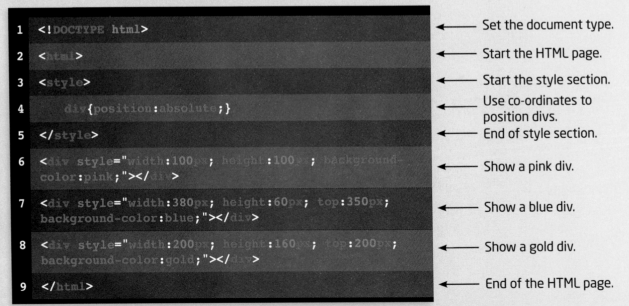

```
1   <!DOCTYPE html>
2   <html>
3   <style>
4       div{position:absolute;}
5   </style>
6   <div style="width:100px; height:100px; background-
    color:pink;"></div>
7   <div style="width:380px; height:60px; top:350px;
    background-color:blue;"></div>
8   <div style="width:200px; height:160px; top:200px;
    background-color:gold;"></div>
9   </html>
```

Set the document type.

Start the HTML page.

Start the style section.

Use co-ordinates to position divs.

End of style section.

Show a pink div.

Show a blue div.

Show a gold div.

End of the HTML page.

STEP 3: Save your page

■ Click **File > Save**.

■ Browse to your documents folder.

■ Type **art.html** as the file name.

STEP 4: View your page

Open your documents folder and double-click the **art.html** file.

documents/art.html

Coders often copy and paste lines of code to save time and avoid mistyping.

STEP 5: Add more shapes - copy some code

Click here to position your cursor at the start of a line.

```
8  <div style="width:200px; height:160px; left:150px;
   top:200px; background-color:gold;"></div>
```

Drag down to highlight the line of code.

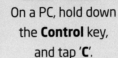

Ctrl C

On a PC, hold down the **Control** key, and tap '**C**'.

cmd ⌘ C

On a Mac, hold the **Command** key then tap '**C**'.

STEP 6: Make space and paste your code

```
9  </html>
```
Click at the start of line 9.

Press the enter key to make a gap.

```
9
10  </html>
```

```
9
10  </html>
```
Click at the start of line 9 again.

Ctrl V

On a PC, hold down the **Control** key, and tap '**V**'.

cmd ⌘ V

On a Mac, hold the **Command** key then tap '**V**'.

Edit line 9 to make a new shape. Change the position, size and colour.

STEP 7: Edit the new line of code

Now you will have two lines with the same code.

```
8  <div style="width:200px; height:160px; left:200px;
   top:350px; background-color:gold;"></div>
9  <div style="width:200px; height:160px; left:200px;
   top:350px; background-color:gold;"></div>
10  </html>
```

STEP 8: See the changes

Save your work again, then refresh your web page. See step 4 on page 17 for help with this and to arrange your screen.

■ EXPERIMENT

Copy and paste more lines of code. Change the colour of each of the new divs. You can use words like lightblue or darkpurple (no spaces). Remember to save and refresh your page to see the changes. Set new values for the width, height, top and left attributes. Read the next page to learn how to use millions of other colours!

How do Screens Display Graphics?

If you look closely at an image on a screen you will see that it is made up of millions of tiny squares - called pixels.

If you look through a powerful magnifying glass you will see that each pixel is made up of three tiny LEDs. These LEDs are red, green or blue.

Mixing colours

We can create different colours by mixing different amounts of red, green and blue light. This is done by making each of the three LEDs slightly brighter or dimmer. The amount of each colour is set by giving it a value. This is called the RGB colour system.

In most HTML pages a number is given between 0 and 255 for the amount of red, green and blue in the colour. This gives over 16 million combinations. The code to show bright red in an HTML page is 255,0,0. The red value is 255, green is 0 and blue is 0. Some other systems use a decimal value between 0 and 1 instead of 0 and 255. This means the code to show red would be 1,0,0.

Don't worry if you don't understand all that yet. Just try using these colour codes and experiment!

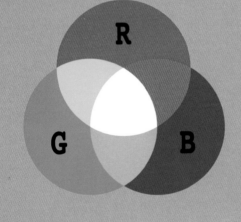

Colour	Red	Green	Blue	Decimal
Red	255	0	0	1 0 0
Green	0	255	0	0 1 0
Blue	0	0	255	0 0 1
Yellow	255	255	0	1 1 0
Purple	128	0	128	0.5 0 0.5
White	255	255	255	1 1 1
Black	0	0	0	0 0 0
Dark Red	204	0	0	0.8 0 0

We will use decimal values when we do some 3D graphics work.

Try making small changes to an RGB code. Compare: rgb (0,0,200), rgb (0,50,200) and rgb (0,100,200)

Now edit your shapes code and try using RGB values instead of colour names.

```
<div style="width:380px; height:60px; top:350px;
background-color:rgb(0,0,200);"></div>
```

Coding 3D Graphics

Now we have learned how to make simple 2D graphics in HTML, let's have a look at creating some 3D graphics.

You can use lots of different methods to design 3D graphics, but we will be looking at how you can use code to do this.

Films are sometimes made in **3D**. You usually need special glasses to watch 3D films. Animated films are partly created by code written in a language called Python. Code is also used to add special effects to 'real' films. This is called **CGI**.

VR - Virtual Reality allows people to interact with objects and environments created by computer code in 3D. You need a special headset to use VR.

AR - Augmented Reality is a way of showing computer generated images on top of 'real' images - through glasses or a phone camera image. Some apps are coded to help people find where things are on a street, or used in games to find monsters!

> Computer games sometimes use simple ways to make things look 3D.

> So far, our HTML code has used two values to position where things went - how far from the top, and how far from the left. Scratch uses x and y values to set how far across, and how far up the screen things are.

> When we work in 3D, we need three co-ordinates. These are the x,y and z values of where objects are. We also need to set their width, height and depth.

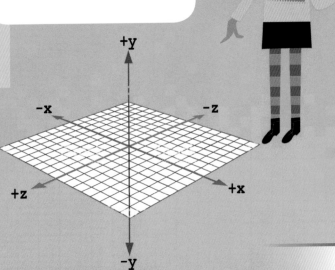

Introducing X3D

Let's add some simple 3D shapes to an HTML page.

To make things simple we will use a code library to help us. This is a bit like using the pen extension in Scratch (see page 6). The library is called X3D. The code library will allow us to use a number of new tags to add 3D shapes to the page, set how big they are, their colour and other values.

> We will add a <script> tag inside the head section to include the X3D code library.

> To keep things organised we will split our HTML page into two sections.

```
<head>
..
</head>

<body>
..
</body>
```

The head contains information about the HTML document and is not visible in the browser.

The body contains the code that generates what is seen in a browser.

> We will use the following tags to add a 3D box to the web page.

<x3d> — The start of the X3D section. This gets the page ready to show 3D, and includes the tags below to set all the details. All X3D sections begin with this tag.

<scene> — A scene can contain a number of shapes.

<shape> — Each shape starts with this tag.

<appearance> — This tag introduces information about what the shape looks like.

<material> — The shape's colour and texture are set here. Instead of using the **color** attribute like normal HTML, we need to use the **diffuseColor** attribute to set the colour. (Diffuse just means the real colour of a 3D object under a white light.) The **diffuseColor** is set using RGB decimal values (see page 20).

<box> — This is where the actual shape is added.

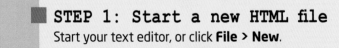

STEP 1: Start a new HTML file
Start your text editor, or click **File > New**.

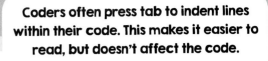

Coders often press tab to indent lines within their code. This makes it easier to read, but doesn't affect the code.

STEP 2: Type in the HTML code

Type this code into your text editor.

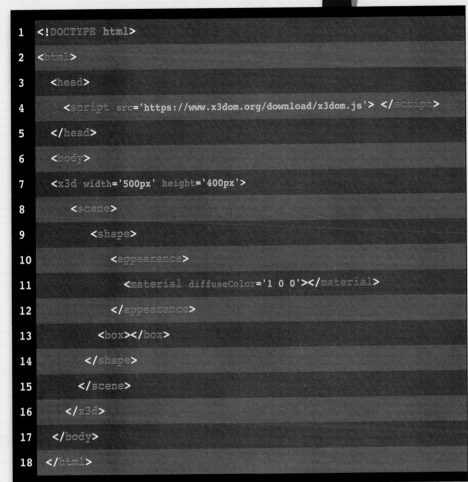

```
1   <!DOCTYPE html>
2   <html>
3     <head>
4       <script src='https://www.x3dom.org/download/x3dom.js'> </script>
5     </head>
6   <body>
7   <x3d width='500px' height='400px'>
8       <scene>
9         <shape>
10          <appearance>
11            <material diffuseColor='1 0 0'></material>
12          </appearance>
13        <box></box>
14      </shape>
15    </scene>
16  </x3d>
17  </body>
18  </html>
```

← Set the document type.

← Start the HTML page.

← Start the head section.

← Include the X3D library.

← End of head section.

← Start the body section.

← Start the X3D section.

← Start the scene.

← Start the shape.

← Describe what the shape looks like. 1 0 0 means full red light, no green and no blue – giving red.

← Draw a 3D box.

← End the shape.

← End the scene.

← End the X3D section.

← End the body section.

← End the HTML page.

STEP 3: Save your page

- Click **File > Save**.
- Browse to your documents folder.
- Type **3d.html** as the file name.

STEP 4: View your page

Open your documents folder and double-click on the **3d.html** file.

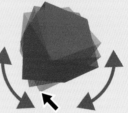

Use your mouse to drag the 3D shape to different angles. Use the mouse wheel to zoom in.

EXPERIMENT

Try out different colours. Change 1 0 0 to 0 0 1. Save your page and refresh your browser. Use the table on page 20 to help you.

Try changing <box> to <cone> or <cylinder>. Remember to change the closing tag too.

X3D Tree

Most objects shown in 3D are built by combining several shapes together. In this next project, we will build a simple 3D tree by combining a brown cylinder and a green cone.

The code will need to set the size of the shapes as well as their colour. It will also need to position them on top of one other.

> Measurements in X3D are bigger than pixels. They don't have an official name but we'll call them units.

> We will need to change the size of the cone and cylinder.

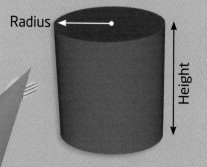

Cylinder

Radius

Height

If you don't set the radius, X3D will set it as 1. This is called its default value. The default height is 2. We will make it thinner, by changing the radius to 0.3.

Cone

Height

bottomRadius

The default height of the cone is 2. The default bottom radius is 1. We will make it taller, by changing the height to 4.

> The transform tag will allow us to position the shapes.

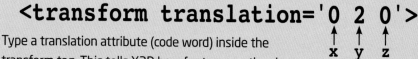

Type a translation attribute (code word) inside the transform tag. This tells X3D how far to move the shape in each of the x, y and z directions (see page 21 for a reminder about x, y and z). The values 0 2 0 mean just move a shape in the y direction, moving it up by 2 units.

STEP 1: Start a new HTML file
Start your text editor, or click **File > New**.

STEP 2: Start coding
Type this code into your text editor.

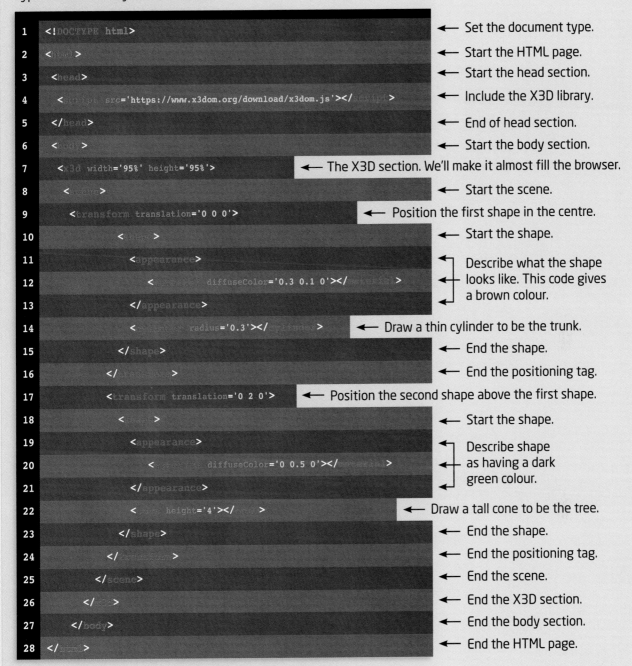

```
1   <!DOCTYPE html>                                          ←  Set the document type.
2   <html>                                                   ←  Start the HTML page.
3     <head>                                                 ←  Start the head section.
4       <script src='https://www.x3dom.org/download/x3dom.js'></script>  ←  Include the X3D library.
5     </head>                                                ←  End of head section.
6     <body>                                                 ←  Start the body section.
7       <x3d width='95%' height='95%'>                       ←  The X3D section. We'll make it almost fill the browser.
8         <scene>                                            ←  Start the scene.
9           <transform translation='0 0 0'>                  ←  Position the first shape in the centre.
10            <shape>                                        ←  Start the shape.
11              <appearance>                                 ┐  Describe what the shape
12                <material diffuseColor='0.3 0.1 0'></material>  ├  looks like. This code gives
13              </appearance>                                ┘  a brown colour.
14              <cylinder radius='0.3'></cylinder>           ←  Draw a thin cylinder to be the trunk.
15            </shape>                                        ←  End the shape.
16          </transform>                                     ←  End the positioning tag.
17          <transform translation='0 2 0'>                  ←  Position the second shape above the first shape.
18            <shape>                                        ←  Start the shape.
19              <appearance>                                 ┐  Describe shape
20                <material diffuseColor='0 0.5 0'></material>  ├  as having a dark
21              </appearance>                                ┘  green colour.
22              <cone height='4'></cone>                     ←  Draw a tall cone to be the tree.
23            </shape>                                        ←  End the shape.
24          </transform>                                     ←  End the positioning tag.
25        </scene>                                           ←  End the scene.
26      </x3d>                                               ←  End the X3D section.
27    </body>                                                ←  End the body section.
28  </html>                                                  ←  End the HTML page.
```

STEP 3: Save
- Click **File > Save**.
- Browse to your documents folder.
- Type **tree.html** as the file name.

STEP 4: View
Open your documents folder and double-click on **tree.html**.

Use your mouse to rotate the tree. Use the mouse wheel to zoom in.

EXPERIMENT
Try changing the height of the cone, and radius of the trunk. Experiment with colours.

X3D Forest

Now let's make a forest by copying and pasting more trees.

STEP 5: Copy the shape code

1. Highlight all the code from line 9 to line 24: from the first **<transform>** tag to the end of the second **</transform>** tag.

Ctrl C — On a PC, hold down the **Control** key, and tap '**C**'.

cmd ⌘ C — On a Mac, hold the **Command** key then tap '**C**'.

STEP 6: Make space and paste your code

Click at the start of line 25.

Press the **Enter** key to make a gap.

Click at the start of line 25 again.

Ctrl V — On a PC, hold down the **Control** key, and tap '**V**'.

cmd ⌘ V — On a Mac, hold the **Command** key then tap '**V**'.

STEP 7: Edit the new tree shapes to move them

We need to change the x value of the transform tag in each of the shapes. Let's move them to the right.

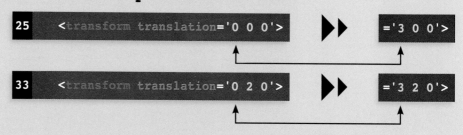

```
25    <transform translation='0 0 0'>    ▶▶    ='3 0 0'>

33    <transform translation='0 2 0'>    ▶▶    ='3 2 0'>
```

STEP 8: See the changes

Save your work again, then refresh your web page. See step 4 on page 17 for help.

■ EXPERIMENT

Try moving the second tree around. Change the values in the transform tag in lines 25 and 33.

Can you add a third tree? Move your cursor to the start of line 41 and make some space. Paste in the tree shapes again. Move the shapes around using step 7 to help you.

How many trees can you add?

X3D Solar System

3D graphics can be used to create models of objects. In this project we will create a 3D solar system with code.

Each planet will be created from a 3D sphere. We'll start with the Sun and the inner planets – Mercury, Venus, Earth and Mars.

We'll need to do some planning to work out how big to make the Sun and each planet and where to put them.

The Sun is much bigger, at 109 R. That's about 109 times the radius of the Earth!

If we made the Sun this much bigger in our model it would be hard to see anything else, so we will just make it three times bigger.

Distances
The Earth is about 150 million km from the Sun. Astronomers call this 1.0 **AU** (Astronomical Unit). Based on that:

Planet	Distance (**AU**)
Mercury	0.4
Venus	0.7
Earth	1
Mars	1.5

Sizes
The radius of the Earth is about 6,400 km. Astronomers call this value **R**.

Planet	Radius (**R**)
Mercury	0.38
Venus	0.95
Earth	1
Mars	0.53

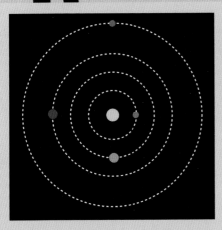

Distances
We will multiply up the distances in AUs by 10, and work out where to put the planets.

Planet	x	y	z
Sun	0	0	0
Mercury	4	0	0
Venus	0	0	7
Earth	-10	0	0
Mars	0	0	-15

STEP 1: Start a new HTML file
Start your text editor, or click **File > New**.

STEP 2: Start coding

Type this code into your text editor.

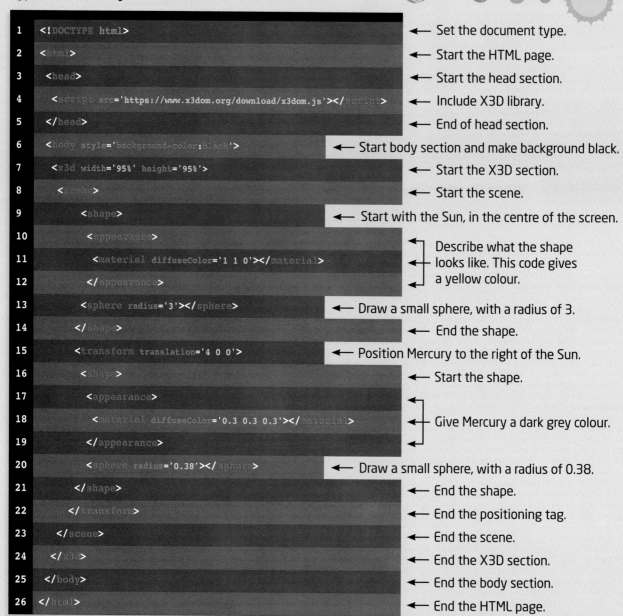

```
1   <!DOCTYPE html>                                          ← Set the document type.
2   <html>                                                   ← Start the HTML page.
3     <head>                                                 ← Start the head section.
4       <script src='https://www.x3dom.org/download/x3dom.js'></script>   ← Include X3D library.
5     </head>                                                ← End of head section.
6     <body style='background-color:black'>                  ← Start body section and make background black.
7       <x3d width='95%' height='95%'>                       ← Start the X3D section.
8         <scene>                                            ← Start the scene.
9           <shape>                                          ← Start with the Sun, in the centre of the screen.
10            <appearance>                                  ┐
11              <material diffuseColor='1 1 0'></material>  ├← Describe what the shape looks like. This code gives a yellow colour.
12            </appearance>                                 ┘
13            <sphere radius='3'></sphere>                   ← Draw a small sphere, with a radius of 3.
14          </shape>                                         ← End the shape.
15          <transform translation='4 0 0'>                  ← Position Mercury to the right of the Sun.
16            <shape>                                        ← Start the shape.
17              <appearance>                                ┐
18                <material diffuseColor='0.3 0.3 0.3'></material>  ├← Give Mercury a dark grey colour.
19              </appearance>                               ┘
20              <sphere radius='0.38'></sphere>              ← Draw a small sphere, with a radius of 0.38.
21            </shape>                                       ← End the shape.
22          </transform>                                     ← End the positioning tag.
23        </scene>                                           ← End the scene.
24      </x3d>                                               ← End the X3D section.
25    </body>                                                ← End the body section.
26  </html>                                                  ← End the HTML page.
```

STEP 3: Save

■ Click **File > Save**.

■ Browse to your documents folder.

■ Type **solar.html** as the file name.

STEP 4: View

Open your documents folder and double-click on **solar.html**.

Rotate the scene.

STEP 5: Copy the Mercury code

Highlight all the code from line 15 to line 22. (From <transform> to after </transform>) then copy the code.

STEP 6: Make space then paste

 `</scene>`

Click at the start of line 23.

Press **Enter**.

`23`
`24 </scene>`

`23`
`24`

Click at the start of line 23 again.

Paste the code in. Repeat steps 1-4 again twice.

STEP 7: Start coding

Edit the pasted code to show the next three planets so it looks like this.

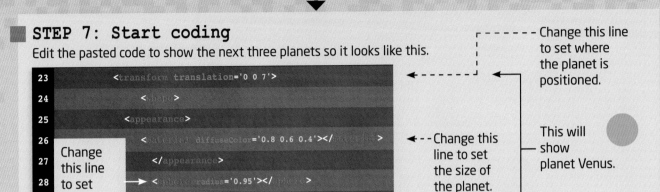

Change this line to set where the planet is positioned.

Change this line to set the size of the planet.

```
23        <transform translation='0 0 7'>
24            <shape>
25            <appearance>
26            <material diffuseColor='0.8 0.6 0.4'></material>
27            </appearance>
28            <sphere radius='0.95'></sphere>
29            </shape>
30            </transform>
31        <transform translation='-10 0 0'>
32            <shape>
33            <appearance>
34            <material diffuseColor='0.2 0.2 0.6'></material>
35            </appearance>
36            <sphere radius='1'></sphere>
37            </shape>
38            </transform>
39        <transform translation='0 0 -15'>
40            <shape>
41            <appearance>
42            <material diffuseColor='1 0.1 0'></material>
43            </appearance>
44            <sphere radius='0.53'></sphere>
45            </shape>
46            </transform>
47        </scene>
48        </x3d>
49        </body>
50 </html>
```

Change this line to set the size of the planet.

This will show planet Venus.

This will show planet Earth.

This will show planet Mars.

This is the code you typed in step 2.

STEP 8: View changes

Save your work again, then refresh your web page. See step 4 on page 17 for help.

EXPERIMENT

Try changing the colours and sizes of the planets. Research the other four planets. Work out how big to make them and try adding them one at a time to your 3D model.

The Scratch Screen

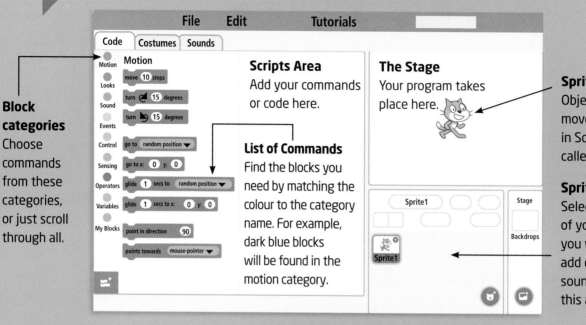

Block categories
Choose commands from these categories, or just scroll through all.

Scripts Area
Add your commands or code here.

List of Commands
Find the blocks you need by matching the colour to the category name. For example, dark blue blocks will be found in the motion category.

The Stage
Your program takes place here.

Sprites
Objects that move around in Scratch are called sprites.

Sprites Pane
Select which of your sprites you want to add code or sound to in this area.

Glossary

3D Graphics
a way to draw objects on a computer to give them a third dimension – depth. For example 2D graphics will draw a circle, 3D graphics will draw a sphere or ball with shading

Algorithm
rules or steps followed to make something work or complete a task

Augmented Reality
images produced by a computer and used together with a view of the real world

Bug
an error in a program that stops it working properly

CGI (Computer Generated Image)
a picture created by a computer. In films this is used to describe computer graphics that are so detailed they look real

Code block
a draggable instruction icon used in Scratch

Co-ordinates
the position of an element using left and top properties to describe how far down and across it is from the top left corner of the page

Debug
removing bugs (or errors) from a program

Element
part of an HTML web page such as text or graphics

HTML (HyperText Markup Language)
a computer language typed into a computer to create a web page

Icon
a small clickable image on a computer

LED (Light Emiting Diode)
a tiny electronic light, combined in hundreds of thousands to create computer screens

Loop
repeating one or more commands a number of times

Pixel
a tiny dot on a computer screen, combined in their thousands to display pictures

Property
information about an HTML element – for example what colour or size it is

Random
a number that can't be predicted

Render
to convert from a file containing code and information describing an image into the image described

Right-click
clicking the right mouse button on a sprite or icon

RGB
stands for red, green and blue and is a system of lights that are mixed to create other colours on a screen

Sprite
in Scratch, an object with a picture on it that moves around the stage

Bugs & Debugging

When you find your code isn't working as expected, stop and look though each command you have put in. Think about what you want it to do, and what it is really telling the computer to do. If you are entering one of the programs in this book, check your have not missed a line. Some things to check:

SCRATCH

Select sprites before adding code:

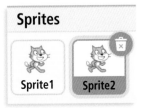

Before you add code to a sprite, click on it in the **Sprites pane**. This will select it and make sure the code is assigned to it.

Right colour, wrong code?

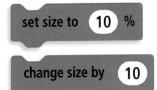

Be precise. Many code blocks look very similar but do completely different things.

HTML

If your HTML code doesn't seem to be working properly, save your code then refresh your browser. Look for clues about where the problem might be.

Look for patterns
The end of line 3 looks different.

Highlighted code
Unexpected code may be highlighted.

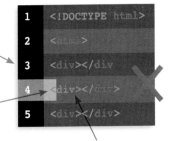

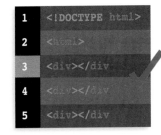

Text colour
This div tag is a different colour.

Here are some other things to check for:

Brackets All the brackets in HTML matter. Make sure your tags have < angle brackets > and are closed with a slash like this </div>. Other parts of your code will have curly brackets { and }.

Semi-colons and colons When you are setting properties check you have used : and ; correctly.

Other symbols Check you have used = and , correctly

Capitals Check you have typed capitals in the way they are written in the book. Most code words need to be lower case (eg **style**), some parts are in capitals (eg **DOCTYPE**) and some are mixed (eg **diffuseColor**).

Spelling mistakes HTML is fussy about spelling mistakes. Don't forget to spell color without a u.

Line numbers When you are copying in long lines of code from this book they may spill over onto the next line. Check each line number of your code, and see if it has the same line number as the one in the book.

Stage
the place in Scratch that sprites move around on

Steps
small movements made by sprites

3D
a three dimensional image showing the depth as well as height and width of an object

Variable
a value used to store information in a program that can change

Virtual Reality
a realistic 3D world created with computer graphics. By wearing a special headset users can look around the world by moving their head around

Index

123
3D effects, create 8-9, 15, 21-29
      using X3D 5, 22-29

A
AR (augmented reality) 5, 21

C
colour, adding 4-6, 11, 20
CGI (computer generated images) 5, 12-13, 21

D
drawing 6-7

E
Engelbart, Douglas 10

G
graphics, history of computer 4-5

H
HTML 5, 15-29

I
images, rendering 5

M
mouse, the first 10

P
painting 10-11
pixels 4, 6, 16, 20
Pong 4

T
text editor, using 14-19, 23-29

V
VR (virtual reality) 5, 21

W
web page, creating a 15-29

Further information

Generation Code: I'm an App Developer
by Max Wainewright (Wayland, 2018)

*Generation Code:
I'm an Advanced Scratch Coder*
by Max Wainewright (Wayland, 2018)

*Get Ahead in Computing:
Amazing Applications & Perfect Programs*
by Clive Gifford (Wayland, 2016)

Project Code series
by Kevin Wood (Franklin Watts, 2017)

Computer Graphics • Drawing with Code • 3D Name • Painting • Special FX • Text-based Coding • HTML Stripes • Shape Art • How do Screens Display Graphics? • Coding 3D Graphics • Introducing X3D • X3D Tree • X3D Forest • X3D Solar System • The Scratch Screen/ Glossary • Bugs & Debugging • Index

Smartphones • Texting • Code Your Own Emojis • Phone Case Design • Building Apps • Web Browser • Location Services • Map App • Camera Technology • Photo Filter App • The Scratch Screen/ Bugs & Debugging • Glossary • Index

Sound and Video • Drums • Recording Sound • Music Keyboard • Simple Music Sequencer • Sound Effects • Text-Based Coding • Adding Video to a web Page • Slow Motion • Pause and Play • Streaming • Embedding Video • Camera Code • Camera Code with Effects • The Scratch Screen/ Glossary • Bugs & Debugging • Index

The Internet • How Data Travels • Editing HTML code • Your Favourites • Colour and Shape • Online Shopping • Links and Photos • JavaScript & Interaction • Moving Around • RGB Colours • Search Engines • Code a Search Engine • Bugs & Debugging • Glossary • Index